MY JOURNEY
with
UNBORN POEMS

Nadakkave, Kozhikode, Kerala, India
www.insightpublica.com
e-mail: insightpublica@gmail.com
My Journey with Unborn Poems
(English Poems)
Vithura V. Asok
Cover design: Midhuna R, Trivandrum
Layout: kjvj@insight
First Edition: July 2021
Copyright©Reserved

ISBN 978-93-91006-36-5
Published and Printed by Insight Publica
for Insightinpublica Printers & Publishers Pvt. Ltd.

₹ 99

MY JOURNEY
with
UNBORN POEMS

(Anthology of English Poems)

VITHURA V. ASOK

With Appreciation by Poet's Son

Vithura. V. Asok (V. Asoka Kumar) was born on 25-03-1966 at Vithura, a remote hamlet in Trivandrum, the Southern-most District in India, as the son of P. Velayudhan Pillai and Kamalamma. He had his education as follows:-

V. V. Daayini U. P. School, Valiyavenkadu (Primary education) 1971- 1978.

Vithura Govt. High School --(High School education) 1978-1981.

Iqbal College, Peringammala. (Higher Secondary & graduation). 1981-1987.

Institute of English, Kerala University (Master's Degree in English Language & Literature) 1987-89.

Mar Theophilus Training College, Nalanchira (Bachler's Degree in Education) 1990-1991.

Institute of Distance Education, University of Kerala (Masters Degree in Public Administration) 1998-2000.

He started official career in Vigilance & Anti-Corruption Bureau, Kerala in 1991and is now working as Administrative Officer in the Bureau.

His wife Suja. P. S, M.A, B.Ed (an official in District Panchayath, Govt. of Kerala, Trivandrum)

A. S. Aswin (Graduate in Mechanical Engineering) and A.S. Aaraj (Graduation Student in English Language and Literature) are his sons.

Residential Address:
Vithura. V. Asok.
(V. Asoka Kumar)
Snehatheertham, Kunnumpuram,
Kulasekaram, Kodunganoor. P. O.
Trivandrum District. Kerala State,
India. PIN Code - 695013.
Contact No. 9496408698. 7025681171.
E. Mail. asokansnehatheertham1966@gmail.com

VITHURA. V. ASOK

DEDICATION

This being my maiden literary attempt, this Anthology is dedicated to the memory of William Shakespeare.

WHY SHAKESPEARE.. ?

Shakespeare, Shakespeare everywhere, why?
The most shaking confusion I faced ever.
In schools, Universities, Books, all academic discourses, why?
Shakespearean characters still live around me, in me too.
The Shylock still in me, as a lending, luring lust,
Romeo still in me, as a passionate, wreckless lover, roaming the Juliets,
Unlucky Othello in me still strangling the loyal lips of Desdemonas,
The back-stab of Brutus, a fatal wound still in my breast, not at my back.
Hamlet still in me, Hamletism my worst wreckful elephantiasis ever,
Unique nose of Cleopatra, the Caesar in me still longue you,
Swelling ambitions in me excel Macbeth in all sorts of treachery.
This isle filled with little Calibans, but Prospero withhold all Tempests.
The great Elizabethan excitement ! everlasting joy of the Globe !!
What a great art, what a great craft, thou myriad characters!!!
Oh! the great Bard, your wards still dance in my blood, breast and brain.

VITHURA. V. ASOK.

ACKNOWLEDGEMENTS

My first and foremost gratitude to my parents, P. Velayayudhan Pillai, my father and P. Kamalamma, my mother, who had only primary education, but struggled a lot to bring me up despite their economically dim and rurally grim background.

My second, but the prime gratitude is to Mr. Joseph Puthiyadom. When the destiny brought me before him in 1982, I was so poor in English Language, scoring less than 10% marks for English in School Examinations and was not confident either to write or speak English. But my two years as his student ignited the sparks of the Language in me, that I did Post-graduation in English Language & Literature, today I write poems in English Language, which are read and appreciated by my Poet-friends (in the Facebook) across the globe. He is still my source of inspiration that prompted me this attempt. It was with great pleasure and in-depth love that he attempted a marvelling Preface to this anthology. My sincere gratitude to him.

It was with studious enthusiasm that my younger son A S. Aaraj (who is a student of the English Language and Literature) attempted a tempting Special Appreciation to this Anthology.

I am also indebted to Mrs. Suja PS, my wife and Mr. A.S. Aswin, my elder son for their motivation and co- operation in this effort.

Kumari Midhuna R. Trivandrum designed the marvellous cover page of this anthology, touching the soul of the poems "My Journey" and "Luminous Orgasm" also my gratitude to her.

My utmost gratitude to M/s. INSIGHT PUBLICA Kozhikode for materializing my long-cherished dream into a beautiful reality, it being my maiden literary venture.

Thanks a lot to all.

JOSEPH PUTHIYADOM
Puthiyadom House,
Amboori. P. O,
Kattakkada,
Trivandrum Dist.
(Principal & Director Institute of English, Vithura)

FORWARD

It's my pride and privilege, so special, to pen this Forward to this Anthology "MY JOURNEY with UNBORN POEMS", a compilation of 40 poems by Vithura V. Asok.

If Miranda is the quintessence of Shakespearian heroines, it is because the creator chose the most beautiful and exquisite elements from the Nature for the creation of that personification of beauty. Likewise Vithura. V.Asok endeavoured strenuously to bring out this Anthology "MY JOURNEY with UNBORN POEMS", following the footsteps of the great masters, adopting their methods, quibbling of words and in choosing themes. Undoubtedly, his poems reflect Wordsworth's pantheism, Coleridge's mysticism, Keat's sensuousness, Robert Browning's robustness as in his Dramatic Monologues, the revolutionary roar of Shelly and the ardent patriotism of Tennyson, all these as in the romantic period of the English poetry. Like Shakespeare this budding poet has "magnanimous mind", he possesses a sharp insight like that of Milton, who had no physical sight. Some of his poems have an affinity to Elliot's candid presentation, Kamala Das' innocent approach, Nissim Ezekiel's mundane touch and Robert Frost's practicality.

I appreciate Vithura V. Asok for exposing a spark of genre to erudite his readers with the ingredients sprinkled over his work. I am also glad to mention that Vithura V. Asok was a student of mine in the 1980's, a diligent, intelligent and an inquisitive student then. May God, the Almighty shower upon him His abundant grace to proceed with the Promethean Art of eternal beauty as well as robust health.

A.S. AARAJ
(S/o the Poet)
B. A. Student, (English Language & Literature)
Mahathma Gandhi College.
Trivandrum.

A SPECIAL WORD OF APPRECIATION

Sometimes, I shall be the first son (or daughter) who tempts or attempts to draft or craft an introduction to a literary work penned by his (or her) own father (or mother). But to me it is not a temptation, but a prompt lured by the fact that I am a student of English Literature. It too a casual coincidence that the poems in this Anthology happened to be penned at my own dwelling, and I got the chance to read them first.

According to my breast and brain as a literature student, many poems in this Anthology seems to be in traditional English poetry lines and tunes, but in free verse. Many of them seem to be a sort of quite, but elegiac revolts against the degeneration and disintegration of the human values in the 21 Century's consumer-oriented lives in "ivory towers". The poems" Poetry, My language", "Brutus", "A Good Fence", "The Beggar" etc tear off the hypocritical masks worn by us in our post modern contemporary society, that too with soft-sharped poetic blades.

The poem "Miss. Universe" transcends the luring beauty of life to the seducing mesmerism of death. "Who is afraid of death?" is the blissful conflict the poem poses, that too a celestial conflict, "to live here more "or "to embrace death, the dazzling beauty princess at once? " The sexual chemistry works out between the life and death forms the aesthetic base of the poem(that too with a meta-physical touch). The poem "My Un-born Brothers" too casts such a broad reading pleasure and perspective.

The poems, "My Journey", " Twinkle Twinkle Little Stars", "Rain Rain Go Away", "Stopping by Woods on a Bright Morning", " Chasing a Cheetah ", ".My Migration", " The Burning Planet", etc cannot be categorised as mere Nature Poems. A supreme blend of the scenic and serene beauty of the Nature with the nostalgic sense of losing bonds of love(the losing love between the Nature and man as well as between the men themselves) weave the basic thread of these poems, that too like sweat-drops oozing out from a phased orphaning of rich human life.

My student-nerves pulse the poems in this Anthology as the impulses of a poet-beggar with a morbid fascination for the hapless. It is up to the readers to gauge or engage the poems in other perspectives. It is also interesting to recall the strange old concept that poets are probably mad with fits of frenzy, who can not withdraw themselves far from the madding crowds ignoble strife. It was at a time when the poets were considered as singers like Orpheus. But the role of the poets in contemporary society deserves to be examined, ie. whether poetic works are for aesthetic appreciation only, or whether the poets are to be a corrective force , not only to point out the wrong-doings and the wrong-doers, but fight them with poetic swords. I think this question, the poetic community across the globe will examine with a serious note.

POEMS

POETRY, MY LANGUAGE

Adam and Eve, no language,
Yet they loved, hand in hand.
Had one language, one word,
The taste of the fore-bidden fruit.

Their sons too, one language, one voice,
Bricks one upon one, a tower at Shinar,
Just a moment, to touch the heaven,
But for God's mischief, myriad languages.

Languages in plenty, we speak,
Native, foreign and vernacular,
Each tribe, each group with its own,
Only swords to fight, no word to love.

Yes, we can count all our bones,
But can't we count all our words,
Our prophecies, our premonitions,
Nagging dreams of a frenzied luncheon.

We Poets, we sing one language,
The chorus of love and oneness.
Our language, our faith, our God,
Our poems, the saga of humanity.

●

MY JOURNEY

Like anyone, my long-cherished dream,
A jolly trip to the distant snowy altitudes,
Down to the lovely valleys, in morning rays,
To the golden shores, in moon-lit nights,
To the Royal Palace, see the lovely Princess,
A jolly trip, a lovely trip, never to forget.

Roots entangled to the depths in deep,
Branches, shelters to the singing chirps,
Shades, cool to the way-farers and destitutes,
Leaves, busy cooking tastes, for one and all,
My long-cherished trip, still al fiasco.

This morning, bright and synergistic, as usual,
The village-man, a wood-cutter, near me,
He fulfilled my long-cherished dream,
A journey to the gorgeous city, of fame and glory,
To adorn the roof of the Royal Palace,
And to see the charming Princess, for ever,
My long-cherished dream, my journey, first and final !
●

BRUTUS...

"Et-tu, Brute! "

Yes, I am Brutus,
You call me Brute,
Yes, l too brute,
But not so brute,

Yes, I stabbed my Lord,
That too, from behind, true,
But one stab, only one stab,
With one stab, l put an end
To the noblest statesmanship, true,
To my unflinching loyalty too.
To stab face to face, I was too frail.

Never l tied knot to any Cleopatra,
Nor to any wild lady of Macbeth,
Ever transcended heredity to none,
But this little STAGE, this little GLOBE,
Full of Brutes, anywhere, any time.

Some in black gowns, full of black lies,
Some in white coats, with venomous prescriptions,
Some in civil, some in uniform,
Some in thrones, with or without crowns,

Some like angels, kissing roses, with thorns,
All mighty or marvellous,
Cute or cunning, but all brutally brute!

They stab, not from behind,
Nor face to face, soft smiles
Their sharp daggers, with colourful masks,
Masks painted with romance or mercy,
So subtle, masking their brute nerves.

Yes, I am Brutus,
Yes I am Brutus!
●

TWINKLE, TWINKLE LITTLE STAR

The great old lady, my grandmother,
   She too had a lovely grandmother,
Who often told sweet, nice stories,
To her grandchildren, every evening.

Her wonderful story, about the stars,
That the men of goodwill on earth,
May rise to the sky, as shining stars,
Always men's virtue, and God's reward.

My grandmother too, with the same story,
And counting the stars, every night,
Never short, all nights, full of joy,
I too amazed at the twinkling stars,

Now I too a grandmother, it's my destiny,
That my grandchildren with no story-time,
And the sky too, without any stars new, for,
Men of goodwill on earth, now rare species.

Now the stars are only in films and politics!
How tragic, to my great grandchildren !
Their sky, and their nights, without stars ???
Only dark horizons, empty of bright stars ???

●

THE CONVICT AND A HANDKERCHIEF

"This convict deserves no mercy,
Hang him unto death,
Hang him unto death "
Pronounced the Judge.
Encomium echoing the Judge's ears,
From the Court Hall, the way out.

"Hang him, not tomorrow,
A callous criminal, "
"Shoot him at once"
"Shoot him at once "
Shouted the aggressive mob,
The powerful final Jury,
Pelting stones, bleeding my forehead.

A gentle cop, extends a hand-kerchief,
To mask my face, from the crazy crowd.
The other cop, eases my hand-cuff,
With left hand, I wipe the sweat on my face first,
And thereafter, my tears too, with my right hand.
"Why this hand-kerchief ?" my broken words.
"To mask your face." the gentle cop.

"To mask my face ?"
Why? Why mask my face?
How to mask my unfaced entity ?
How to mask my defaced identity ?

Sweat and tears simultaneously ?
Why? And why ?And how? It know not.
Sweat, not due to panic of the snooze,
Tears, not due to repentance, that I know.
My blood frozen, oozing sweat
And tears simultaneously.

My face and this hand-kerchief !
●

A PRECIOUS GIFT OF THE TIME

A meteoric miracle from a far away milky way,
Flashed into the golden shore at Rameswaram ,
On the moon-lit night of 15 October 1931,
Baptised with the cosmic WINGS OF FIRE,
From Rameswaram to Thumba he flew,
And from Thumba, to the Mughal Gardens.

Science his religion, humanity his faith,
Thoughts and dreams his propellants,
Visions and missions his satellites,
Man of missiles or the Missile Man ?
Loved man and missiles alike, as none did.
Missiles for men, and not men for missiles !

"We dream while we sleep " said Sigmund Freud.
"Dreams keep us not to sleep " he said.
With unleashing power, he ignited young minds,
Inspiring the children with LUMINOUS SPARKS,
BORN TO BLOSSOM, blossomed dreams in to action.

Music a Science, Science a music
Dreams too music, music to infinity,
Defeated none, but won all.
Thirst for knowledge, quest for humanity.
Scientist, humanist, teacher, million minds ignited.

No eclipse to hide this moon, a scorching moon !
Love to moon, like love to the nation.
"Is this face that launched thousand missiles ? "
His head held high,
his thoughts from clear stream of reason,
His mind without fear,
A personification of Tagore's prayer.
Rich in visions, rich in missions,
Lived a life none could ever,
" THE YOUNGEST INDIAN " ever lived.

The chilled dusk at Shillong,
In the twilight of 27 'nth July 2015,
Teaching his last lesson to the luminaries of tomorrow,
Flashed to another milky way, with thousand missions.
A precious gift of the time!

●

Note:-
1. Rameswaram- the birth place of Dr. A.P.J.Abdul Kalam
2.Thumba:- place where Dr. Kalam started his official career as space scientist.
3.Mughal Gardens :- the official residence of the President of India.

"MISS. UNIVERSE"

Strange enough, strange enough,
Absolutely strange enough,
I fell in love with her, in deep love, of an unusual fathom.
She too loves me ? I know not.
She, the Miss. Universe.

Up in all the ramps,
In all counties, across the countries,
Over the continents,
In all the beauty contests,
With her beaming cosmic beauty,
Beating all the contestants.

Her zig-zag moves, catching cat-walks,
Melting complexion, dark and wild,
Black eye-brows, arches to deadly romance,
Her silver eyes, personification of sublimity,
Wild smiles, adorning her lips always.
Silent, but her notes musical,
FINEST OF ALL THE BEAUTIES EVER !

Strange enough,
I fell in love with her.
A blind, but ecstatic romance!
A rare one, a mystic one.

Her ardent charm, seducing me in dreams,
Over thousands of sleepless nights.

Clad in silky rays of the silver star,
She will come, at the dim solitude
Of a chilled early morning,
On a white horse, she, my dazzling Princess, j
My own dazzling Princess.
She will come, one winter morning.

And will embrace me,
With a mesmerizing kiss, and,
Slowly, slowly, and slowly,
My cardinal instinct ejaculated,
Her lips inter-locked with mine,
Sucking forth my soul, unto the
Highest depths of eternal infinity,
Of the long-cherished ecstatic orgasm,
That too in the dim solitude
Of a winter early morning!

Strange enough, I love her,
My sweet-heart, I wait you,
For long, I wait for you.

●

Just a word.
Death, to most humans,
is the most panicky or fearsome one. To most,
sex is the most fantastic and fascinating activity.
I often feel that Death is the most fantastic
and fascinating sexual activity.
Hence these lines.
About the finest of all the beauties ever.
(cardinal instinct - affinity towards Death).

CRIME AND PUNISHMENT

An intellectual idiot,
Not of Dostovskian talent,
Yet, I write this CRIME,
And this PUNISHMENT too.
My life, so subtle, but
As of never, a DIVINE TRAGEDY.

Severest of the crimes?
To be born in THIS world !
Severest of the punishments?
To live in THIS world!. This life,
HIS GIFT, my RIGHT, for others WRONG !

This life, sweet or bitter?
Sin or sacrifice? boon or bane ?
Not I know, yet,
I laud this LIFE, a precious FILE,
Through yesterdays and todays.
Tomorrow ? Not I know.

Not sun, yet burning for others.
Not Star, yet twinkling for kids.
Not moon, yet shining for lovers.
Not Ocean, yet nurturing pearls and pebbles
At the depth of my deep currents.

Not a cloud, yet wandering lonely
High above, across the blue borders of the horizon.
Not a volcano, yet erupting fiery magma,
Along the tranquil valleys of my beloved.

God's own image, yet begging.
Baking romance in the oven of my heart,
Romance too a crime?
Wed-lock it's punishment ?
A life-term conviction?

Life and Romance, Divine Crimes?
With Divine punishments?
Yet, I love this Life, and this Romance too,
And longing a rebirth at this shore,
A rebirth at this lovely shore.
●

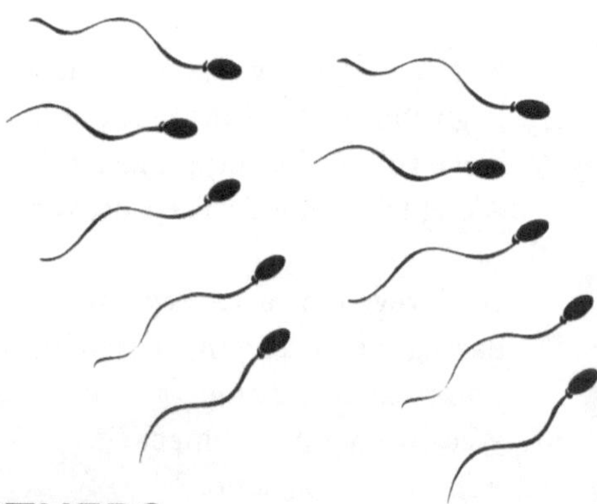

MY UNBORN BROTHERS

Like this Universe, like this Life,
Science too, wonderful,
Medical Science, yet amazing,
One drop of semen contains,
Sperms, not one or two , but one and a half crore !.
Each mating, my father had with my mother,
Emanated sperms not one or two, i
But crores in eight or nine !
Nine crores leaping so fast,
To fuse with the ovum in my mother's womb,
One ,defeating the other nine crores,
With in one out of ten thousand of a second !
How wonderful ! How amazing !
Like the first drop of a rain touching the surface of the earth!
My brothers ? Or sisters ?
Not one or two, but nine crores at a time,
Thousand crores during my father's life - span, '
Run out or swim out in to oblivion,
That too, within ,one out of ten thousand of a second !
What a Puzzle? What an Enigma !

How blessed is my birth, and my life too!
That POWER ,that choose me to be born,
Out of nine crore, and pushed me to win ,
Within one out of ten thousand of a second,

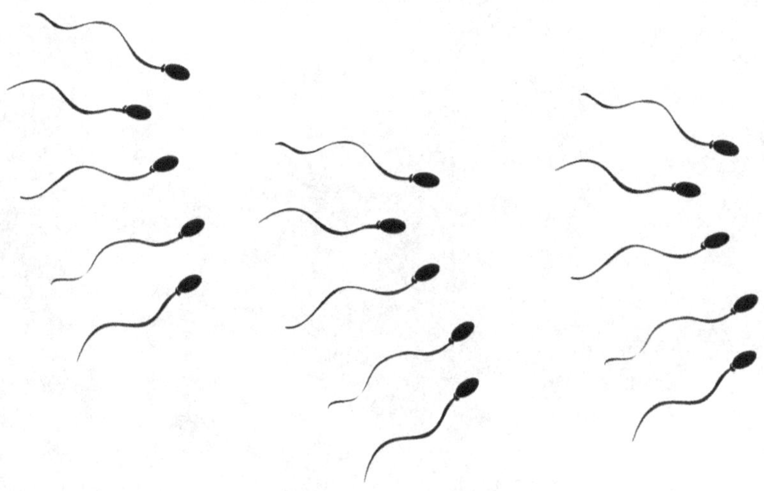

That POWER is my only God !
Others, only mere idols for worship !

My brothers? Or sisters,
Not one or two, but thousand crores,
Swim out in to oblivion, unborn !
Thousand crores swim out, i run out!
My unborn brothers? Or sisters ?
If I were one among them ?
Swimming out into oblivion !
Not seeing this Sun, this Moon, this Earth?
With out this birth, without seeing this world ?
How shocking ? How horrible?
On one half, I feel paralysed !
On the other, ecstatic of this precious birth !

My unborn brothers, not one or two!
But thousand crore ,
Their eyes blue or sparking ? ?
Similar to that of mine ??
Their nose, nail and hair like mine ??
Strength of their hands and power of their legs like mine ??
Their notes , musical like mine ??

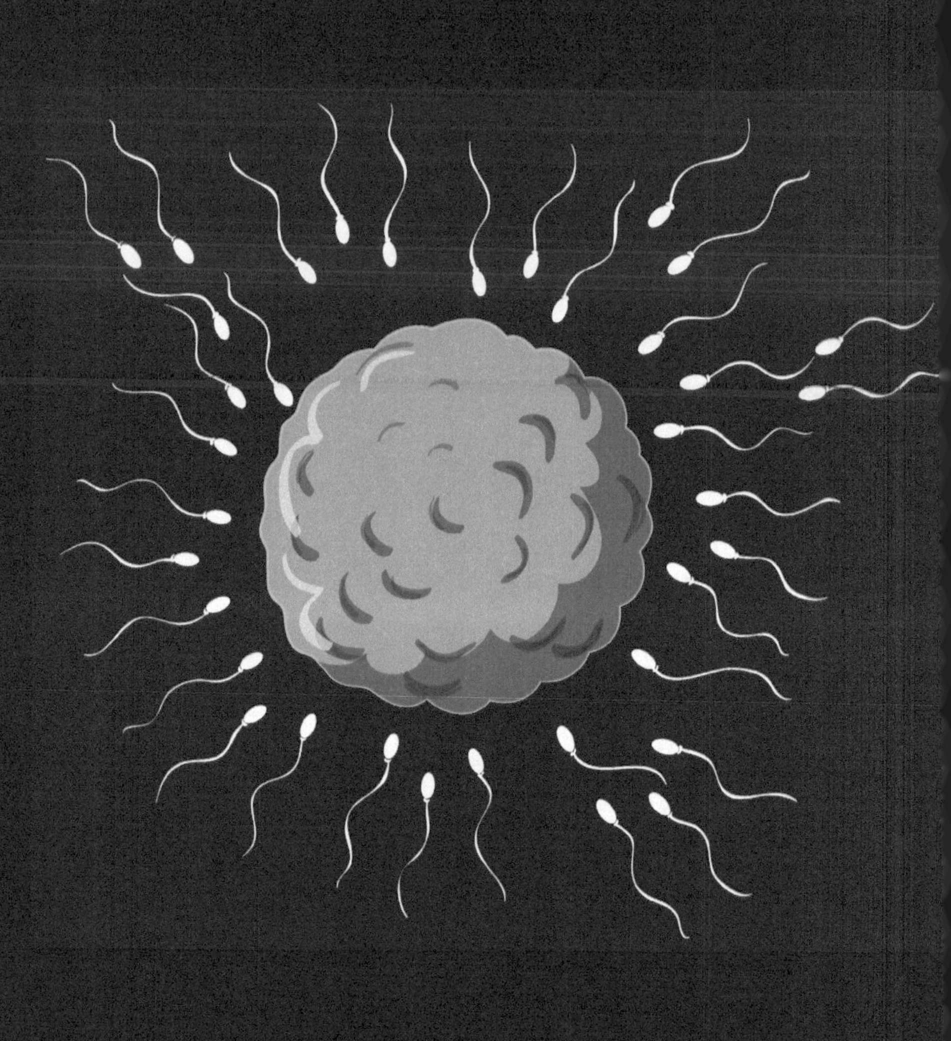

My unborn brothers !Or sisters !
Not one or two, but thousand crores
Swim out into oblivion ! Wow !

On this no- moon morning,
A shivering bath, in the chilled waters,
Of this pious river, the 'Ganga',
I in wet dress, to offer obituary,
To the departed souls of my ancestors and the beloved ,
Submitting the offerings,
A gentle breeze, pat my shoulders ?
May be my unborn brothers Or sisters?
Oh!!! What I to offer to you?????
 For this precious birth and life of mine ?
At the cost of your lost birth !
At the cost of your lost life to o!
My unborn brothers ! Or sisters !
This little drop of my tears,
That too, without any pretention,
Oozing out from the deep depth of my soul, '
This is my obituary, this is my offering,
My unborn brothers ,my unborn sisters,
For your divine Sacrifice to me !
This one drop of tears !

●

THIS LAND, MY MOTHER

Ancient land of great truths ,of great knowledge,
Her head, as high as no peak could ever hold.

Her sons, her daughters, always fragrant flowers
Of myriad colours, not even at heaven,
For, this the most beautiful heaven,
Created by the God, and crafted by her children.

Her tri-colour flag, a unique dream bloomed
From the sagas of million hearts of this precious soil.
High and high, not up to the Lunar shade alone,
Let us hoist this pride on the last shining star too
Of this Milky Way, that its divine fragrance and human touch
May make even the black-holes in to lands of love.

Like the Sun shines to make our land synergic,
Like the Moon brightens our nights off darkness,
Like the Clouds pour elixir of life upon this land,
Let us shower love, self-less love, upon our motherland.
●

(Just a word. A humble tribute and a rich salute to my Nation, India.)

STOPPING BY WOODS ON A BRIGHT MORNING

Whose woods are these ? Mine, my own.
My winged friend's too. Day and night
We linger under these green shades,
Our winged dreams, fly high and high.

Wow ! How synergic this morning too !
 Behind the steep, green eastern hills
Bright rays spreading their arms
To embrace each tender leaf.
My twittering friends fluttering wings,
Like little kids in their mother's lap.
Boundless love from the mother Nature
Spills over from the springs of serenity.

My sweet-heart, my yellow Birdy,
Her zigzag turns, her swift leaps
From one stem to another, and my eyes
Tune new melodies, blend new symphonies.

Her eyes here and there for a worm
Or for a bit of nut or savoury nectar.
My heart chanting thrilling mirth
Of wild ecstasy beaming from these woods.

●

A GOOD FENCE

My school bag, loaded with books,
Mathematics, Chemistry, Philosophy.
Moral lessons class, smart teacher,
"Good fences make good neighbours".

Back home, the Bible, " Love your neighbour",
The Geeta, the Quran too teach the same.
To love my neighbour, for a strong love,
With thick iron-rods, a good fence I made.

Only between the fence, I peep to his kitchen,
And tress-pass his modesty, scratch his nose.
Not only today, but all days . For what ?
The fence is good ? .I, a good neighbour too ??

●

THE BEGGAR

In the streets, here, there, anywhere,
Beggars, I see daily, in numbers,
Same faces, same frames, all lean and pity,
Begging a coin, or a bowl of food,
Or for a piece of cloth or for shelter.
Who is the greatest beggar? I still confuse.

Sweet or milky offerings by devotees,
Offering-Boxes, with coins spilled-over,
Coins, all in gold or silver, countless,
Even the wooden-cross turning gold.
All temples, mosques, churches full. yet,
Who is the greatest beggar? the flash in me !

The God, the greatest trillionaire, or above,
 Yet, HE, still begs, the greatest beggar !
 Dawn to dusk, before the holy places,
In royal streets, in country -roads,
Where -ever four people or four roads meet,
The only beggar, with divine face,

My gentle query, "YOU ?, and why YOU ? "
His gentle tone, as of all beggars,
" Yes, I beg, I beg nothing but humanity,
That I created in abundance,
In all humans, that make them humans,

Like filling deep oceans with water.
No ocean evaporated up to bottom till,
But no drop of humanity, in anyone."

I too in despair, for my pocket too empty,
With no coin of humanity, even of a rust-iron,
The God continues, the greatest beggar !
The only beggar, with divine face !
●

THE ROAD TAKEN

The great Poet sang about THE ROAD NOT TAKEN,
It was years, years ago. I too often confused,
Which road to be taken, whether the Frosty one ?
The road full of dry leaves, not taken by many ?
Roads, roads, around me, not one or two,
To add my woes, three hundred and sixty,
One road each opening at each degree.

At a fragile moment, I opted this one,
Tempted by the fragrance of her foot-prints !
Not even a single rose, but full of thorns only.
Never tempted further, neither tired any how,
Finally I reached this street, at a weary moment,
Where flash-lights, like fire-flies, wink
And the way-farers, to and fro, all in rush.

This junction, not my ultimate destination,
But "full of sounds and furies", all feel merry,
Drinking beers, dancing cheers, sharing joys.
My journey, no my pilgrimage destined,
Not to any holy places, but to this jolly junction,
Where I feel elated and blessed than any where,
No abode, no wine will make me so fine, so merry.

●

THE BURNING PLANET

The great poet, his words so worth,
Called me mother, the Mother Nature.
Yes, I am mother, the mother of all .
With no lust, no greed, I delivered,
And nurtured all my off springs alike.
My breasts feed milk so sweet
And delicious, not just a diet, but elixir.
The elixir to all the life pulse on this planet.
Snakes swallow frogs, tigers beat deers,
Just of hunger, not of taste, I thought.
But my sons killing each other, not of hunger,
But of lust, their lust, ludicrous and lucrative
Now a great fire, that burn my breasts.
These green forests, my heart-vessels
This burning fire, not sparks, but,
Flames of lust recessive in my sons,
Even maternal love can't subside, so violent,
So fierce a fire too, that my head down
With utmost shame to feed my breast,
To such inhuman humans to be my sons.
Don't call me mother, though my heart
Still beat for you and my breasts
Still emulate the divine elixir to you all.

●

ETERNAL LOVE

My first love, to motherhood,
the pulse of all the life on the Earth,
Now a father of two kids, yet my heart still beats
With sublime sweetness of breastmilk, the elixir of all tips of life.

My second love to my father, you call it paternal love,
My mind still thrust with paternal touch in abundance,
To all the beloved sons and daughters born at this shore.

I love all the brothers and sisters, noble fraternal love.
The same thrust of life in all beings, I feel, I heal, I love,
Unique my love mesmerizing, and you praise it Universal love.

When I blend the hidden wild instincts in my deepest depths
With life, my sweetest sweet-heart, you abuse it Erotic love.
But I swear, my love to her, blind but a supreme divine blend,
Blend of Maternal, Paternal, Fraternal, Universal and Erotic,
Never of any lucrative lust, but of pure, pure, sublime love,
For, she is our mother, the mother of eternal Love that surges us forward.

●

RAIN, RAIN GO AWAY

Long ago, it was under an umbrella on a rainy morning,
With my sweet sweet grandma, my first journey,
To the kindergarten, just a few, few miles away,
My grandma, holding me close to her chest.

Hi, the kindergarten, the kids, all budding roses,
Teachers, all caring, personifications of maternal love,
No cradles, no lullabies, but nursery rhymes echo the walls,
"Rain rain go away, come again another day, little Johnny wants to play".

My grandma, like her lullabies, now a sweet memory.
No kindergarten, a sky-scraper to echoes the horns of motor carts.
My mind too a weary desert, sans clouds, sans rain, sans dew-drops,
My hamlet now a metro, here men and wheels too in rush.

All in a sudden, like a day-dream at this lazy-noon,
The sky churning with dark clouds, oh great!
A hurricane, reclamation of my golden childhood memories???
These clouds, showering deep to my green pastures.
That old sweet nursery rhyme, my lips whisper not,
But clamour, "Oh! rain, Oh! rain, come, come again this way".
"Come down, come down, come down shower upon me."
Each drop in me you shower, not rain, but a wet nostalgic Spring,
Or an ocean with ecstatic under-currents of piercing memorabilia !!!.

●

MY TEARFUL JOY

Da Vinci, centuries ago, blended a Code,
And a beautiful portrait. No, a great poem.

Her face glad or gloomy, no critic, no reviewer could explore.
A great genius Shaking Spear across the Globe,
"Full of sounds and furies", to him means nothing.

But to me not an idiotic tale. To be or Not to be,
But the Brutus still ecstatic to stab from behind.

A lonely cloud still wanders high over the valleys of the Helicon,
And the inward eye of the Daffodil still zooms
All the bountiful beauty of this golden lake in a Stolen Boat.

Beyond every Autumn, every Winter, a tumultuous Spring
Flashes colourful joy with mesmerizing fragrance.

The first epic too, a gentle pat on the wounds of the love-bird.
My melodies, heard or unheard, still reverberate
Supreme piety or utmost human penuries in unique passions.
All my tears, reflect rays of sadful joy or joyful sadness.
●

(My Poem dedicated to " WOMANHOOD " across the world)

WOMEN, MYTH or TRUTH ?

1

The rib of Adam? the primitive, great divine myth !
The tender Nature meant only to mate with the Masculin Arrogance?
A beaming wine-glass thrown broken with an empty oral triple talaq.
Myths after myths, all plentiful but painful too, no scarcity !!
But none see the truth, who a Woman is, no what She is !!!
Synonyms, not a handful, but a lot. Mother, grandmother, sister,
Lovely daughter, hottest love or sweetest wife, all angelic figures,
Incarnation of maternal elixir showered to all in plenty.
All He chants, only to conceal His hypocrisy and Her plight.
Yet She fills the wine-glasses of life with love, for one and all.

2

Is She smiling ? or her heart throbbing with agonistic suffocation ??
The perplexing, puzzling smile of Mona Lisa, that is what a Women is !!!
In her eyes, you see only twinkling stars, not her oozing tears,
At her lips you see only drooping cherries, not her whispering agonies,
A marvellous romantic rose, the poets muse in melodies,
Woman, what a beautiful word!! but no man knows her meaning.
A "Consumer-Beauty-Product" in markets and rackets,
Only to be out-raged or molested by the deformed erotic lunatics.
That is woman to men, and He finds nothing else more.
Woman, a great myth or a terrible truth ??? She knows not.
Woman, the great beautiful truth, but born at this lunatic wasteland.
●

TODAY, NOT TOMORROW

All my dreams,
sweet and colourful,

I wake to my feet,
Miles and miles to go.

Yesterdays, with toil and tears
Tomorrows, vague and rough.

Just my shadow, in her eyes,
Shocked to see the" Me" in me.

I am not I am, but another,
I too, JANUS, with two faces.

My back-face, weary but
Measuring the roads chased.

My front -face, dreaming Cleopatra,
And the long-cherished Spring.

Never I taste the fruits of today,
Nor any taste, what so ever.

Bitter yesterdays, untasted tomorrow,
Till I see my shadow, in her eyes !!!
●

LIFE A CIRCUS

Dawn to dusk, dusk to dawn at this stage,
On the roof of life, a rough concrete roost.
My wrinkled face masked with a mascot,
The glamorous mascot of baffling buffoonery,
Called life, always a circus, a balancing act,
Between the right and wrong, my two legs.
My right leg boosted by elegant tempting dreams,
And the left crippled by elephantiasis of stark realities.

These balancing steps between the Satan and the sea,
Often caught between the angelic beauties of life and death.

Call me a clown, or a comic emperor or a buffoon.
Neither lunatic, nor insane, these insatiable mimics,
All these adventures, only for my two inch stomach.

To the stomachs over-loaded with nutritious sandwich of luxury,
My circus may feel wonderful comedy, what a great pity !!!
But to me, it is not a tale told by an idiot, though I, an idiot.
●

MY DAUGHTER

Twenty four years ago, a misty morning,
I too at my twenty four, on a morning walk,
The village road, near-by meadows, grazing cattle's,
In a sudden, a mild groaning, of a new-born baby.

Serene like the morning dew-drop, an infant, blind too.
Abandoned by someone, I embraced her,
To my chest, to my heart, my daughter, my own.
A cradle, in my bosom, I set for her, though I not a lady.

Twenty four years, just twenty four seconds, magic flights.
The smokes in my kitchen, blended unique tastes,
My doctor, torched off her blindness, with sweet vision.
My books, sweet appetites to her passionate thoughts.

Twenty four hours, to betroth her, now a rose, an angelic beauty,
To a groom of her choice, a college lecturer, in the distant city.
Tomorrow morning she will leave me for ever, for ever,
Leaving me in this desert, to the dunes of loneliness to bury me.

Forty eight years, a batchelor's treads, weary like a desert,
She, my daughter, my DEW-DROP, my only mirage or miracle?
She will leave me tomorrow forever, forever she will leave,
But my paternal joy, surpassing my paternal pains, my BOUNDLESS JOY.

●

THE SOUL OF A ROSE

I am ROSE, you call me which ever name,
I am ROSE, you kiss my sweet fragrance.
See the beauty of my rosy petals, unique,
Not sip my nectar, I synthesized for the flies.

Your fingers wounded ? For, my thorns sharp ?
And bleeding like the hearts of the poets ?
My petals, my thorns and my fragrance,
Like poet's smile, laugh, lament and shout.

The lovers, so mad with my fragrance,
The Poets too lunatic with my serene beauty.
Like a dazzling Princess, I dance in the gentle breeze,
Wow ! personification of aesthetic beauty, your kiss, at my soul.

●

CHASING A CHEETAH

Caught between the shining silver stars,
And the dark rays of the neon lamps,
A swift flash over the Niagara falls,
Leaping between the skyline Oak trees
In the rain-forests of the African wilderness,
Chasing a cheetah, to catch it's wild strength,
Neither my iron legs, nor of the cheetah
Ever weary, but with fierce strength we leap.

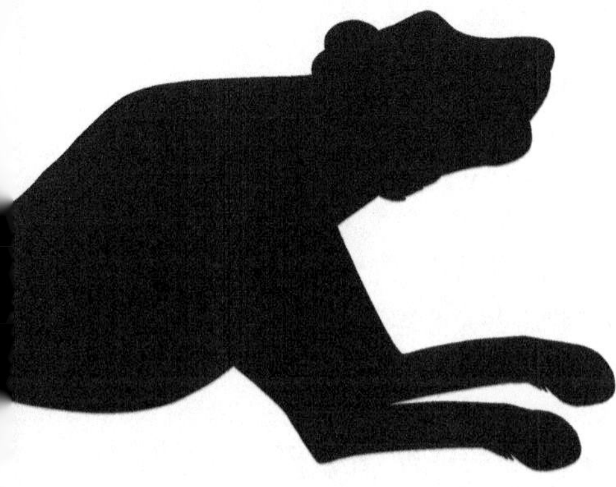

Unwilling to yield, a thousand fathom I chase.
All in a sudden, just at my fingertip,
But with a meteoric jump beyond the dark greenery,
He wins, leaving a handful of spurs to me.
A gentle breeze withering them away,
At the aesthetic hearts as sweet melodies.
Mirage or miracle? but a blend of marvellous tunes!

●

THIS SPRING, AN ANGEL

From where this gentle breeze, this fragrance spring up?
The last night too, that zombie, hoary horrible winter,
Crippled my dreams, rubbing my cheeks with her chilled palms.

Dry grey leaves and the disgruntled wild owls,
Empty stomach, and insomniac, irascible nights,
Sorrows, sorrows, burying me so deep in despair.

From where this gentle breeze, this fragrance spring up?
Oh ! the luxurious, savoury Spring, Oh ! you reach my hut !
To alleviate my sorrows and cleanse my cancerous memoirs,
With your unique, ethereal, angelic healing touch.
This feast of blossoms, these drooping branches.

Your tempting fair frowns, your dew-pearled smiles,
Chirping Cuckoos and the dancing Daffodils,
A brave new heaven with all its gorgeous splendour,
Land in my valley, and my dreams ripe for harvest,
My sorrows dash to graze at the Summer meadows.

●

THE BLUE EYES

The blue ocean with undercurrents of fierce love,
The blue sky so calm and serene, with no clouds,
The blue moon with gentle rays of rare romance,
Never my dear, so piercing to me as your blue eyes.

Your virgin blue eyes bloom a wonderful Spring,
No hills or valleys ever bore so marvellous a feast,
My lonely ways, now lovely track of leaping horses,
Tempting dreams tossing roses on my brooding hopes.

Neither your promised kisses to be jewels on my lips,
Nor your un-lending embraces my eternal ecstasies,
Your synergistic blue eyes mining the virginity of my love,
Two blue lakes quenching my scorching thirst for a erotic blend,
But the orbs in this pool reflects me, a Narcissus so cute.

●

LUMINOUS ORGASM

1.

The summer sun bid audio beside the western sea,
The evening star shy or shining, I see.

The bright clouds, the sprangling twilight, so nice,
The dew-wetlands and the dark jungle paths,
All jubilant with the magic of the evening miracle, the fire-flies.

The luminous stars somehow fell down?
My Maggie, my little daughter too so elated,
With the magic fire-flies, kissing her cheeks,
And some tangling with her curly black hair.
And my memories, rolling back to her mother, my Juliet.

2.

My Juliet and me, just wedded couple, overjoyed,
A thrilling honeymoon trip to the distant Highland moors,
Her lips launching a thousand kisses, our joy spilled over.

The chilling twilight, but with an unexpected guest,
My long-time classmate, mischievous Marvel,
Now a renowned zoologist, and an ardent insectologist.

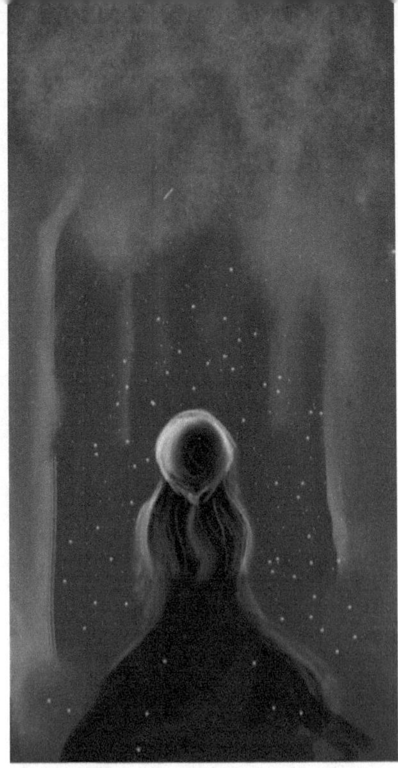

His naughty lecture, a delicious blend,
"You know, the fire-flies and their magic miracle,
Their luminous winks, their mating signals, signals for sex,
The Chemistry of their luminous love, oxidizable luciferin,
And some lady-flies eat their mates, like callous spiders".

A great lesson, no a great revelation, my Juliet elated,
Now an ardent fan of the fire-flies, her joy no bounds.

Each evening, she and the fire-flies, their wonderful world,
On the window bars, or out in the aromatic garden,
Her fingertips elated with the erotic sparks of luciferase,
Her baffling winks, like the fire-flies, her fluorescent kisses,
Our moments, our nights, touch the peaks of luminous orgasm.
Now a foregone Spring, my Juliet, only her fragrant memoirs.

I too miss the firefly magic, and it's luminous touch,
Like an evening lantern, her sparks, illumine me still, a bit.

SOME TIMES,
I MAY NOT BE ALIVE FOR LONG

Sometimes, I may not be alive for long,
But truth and non-violence, the sole elixirs of divility,
Will surge, will survive, will excel all the tests of TIME,
Though, they from my fragile lips, from my frail frame.

Like Desdemona, my dreams strangled to painful death,
My Experiments with Truth, being engraved as epitaphs of humanity,
Swaraj and self-reliance, still tempting wild fiasco.
Love and humanity, only exercises from cosmetic lips.

My mission to see one and all on earth as men,
But my tragic fate, you clitched me 'Mahatma '
No man anywhere, only digits everywhere,
Money and market pervade all walks of life.

You ritualised me, you canonized me,
You idolised me, my statues erected at each cross-road.
My glowing face minted and marketed on currencies.
I had a dream, but you shut it in a marvellous coffin.

Gurudeva's prayer too damned to the hell of devils,

Humanity fragmented by the barriers of regions and religions.
No Master to strike to at the penury of the million hearts.

Now a forgotten figure, down my statues,
Erect the statutes of noble human values and love,
Be good Samaritans, no religion higher than truth.
Some times, I may not be alive for long, but
Truth and Non-violence will surge, will survive for long.
●

(A humble tribute to the father of my Nation, Mahatma Gandhi.)
"Sometimes, I may not be alive for long" – a sentence by Mahatma Gandhi
to a foreign journalist just a few days before his assassination.

MY MIGRATION

A Siberian crane of the Ice-Age, born at winter roosts
My skeleton buried under the snow-drifts behind the Urals.
The magical mystery of the cold winter
Won't warm my dreams, only dark rays above.

Aesthetic hearts muse me "all time wonder "
" The most charismatic white ghosts in the mist ".
" A sacred bird doing penance to the Sun "
Often chant the celestial ripples of the Ob.

Upon the wings of the migration waves,
My distilled journey with a begging bowl
For the warmth of the solar latitude.
The valley of the holy Ganges my warm abode.

Immersing my heads entirely in snow-free water,
My penance to warm my divine eggs, to save
The Siberian wonder from impending catastrophe.
My Spring migration lured by the wetlands far and near.
●

A poem dedicated to the Siberian crane that faces the threat of extinction.
1.--- Urals____The mountain ranges at Siberia.
2. __The Ob__The iced river in Siberia.

AN ANKLET'S DREAM, MINE TOO

Like the wuthering laughters of the gentle streams,
Dancing down to the valley through the forested hillside,
With so hilarious and rhythmic melodies,
Every morning the sweet tunes of my anklets,
Wake me up from my dreams, My lovely anklets.

Though not of golden stuff, of poor but shining silver
From my morning walk to school with my friends,
Never this silk skirt, my mom's precious birthday gift
Neither these golden bangles, my Dad's love gift,
But these anklets, my beloved friends and playmates in dreams too.

Like a little stream dances and dances up to the sea,
Me and my anklets blend same tune, same rhythm, same step,
Will dance and dance from ecstasies to ecstasies,
With the cosmic tunes of this lovely rain, this lonely rain,
Till the last cloud showers down, till the last drop of this lovely rain,
Till my heart breath it's last, till the tender thread of my anklets break.

●

BY THE SEA, DEEP IN THE SEA

Hot waves at the urban streets
Burning my begging foot-steps.
Here each gentle wave at my feet,
What a heeling touch ! by the sea.

Time and tide waited a lot for me,
My deaf ears blind to the musing tides,
My blind eyes deaf to the colours of Time.
Deserted by me to wait , time and tide
Hide in nearby honey-moon cottage,
Shaded by the drooping grapevines.

This vast shore and that deep sea,
With precious preachings in abundance,
The teary, weary life on my shoulders
Always holding me back in her bundle.

Caesarean death diping my meandering remains
Here in the sea, the deep undercurrents
And the beaming corals at the bottom down,
Sniff at me, how I lost the precious pearls
And the ecstatic serene tranquility of this shore
My friends cherish with sweet memoirs.

●

CATCH A FALLING STAR

Watch, watch a rising star,
Then catch the falling star.
Watch a flashing meteor
Then catch the fleeing metaphor.

In a starry moonlit night,
Upon a golden height,
My little mind curious,
Watching stars serious.

A little star above twinkles,
My eyes below wrinkles,
My finer-tips flying so high,
And kissing the star so shy.

Lovely mother pulls me down,
Moonlit meadows take me hidden,
The little star breaks down,
Her tears shower in sudden.

She loves me so deep,
The friendship so we keep,
She, the star falls down,
My laps catch her in sudden.

My heart, my hands get her,
So glad, we shine together.
We leap, we laugh down here,
Other stars, wheels high there.

●

TRAFFIC JAM, GOOD BYE

My heart beats, at seventy -
    two per second,
My lungs jammed with
    exploding suffocation,
My legs frozen with Siberian
    minus seventy,
My burning destination, nearby
    "SUPERMAN'S" hospital.

My daughter, yet to see
    seventy-second full-moon,
My lone daughter, her arteries
    at artful failure.
My friend, her cardiologist,
    with final red alert,
My bag with her rescue valves,
    just seventy minutes left.

My fire, no cloudburst will subside,
    but clearing this traffic- jam,
My fear, who will ? and how? all
    roads widened, but ?
My road, the road I taken, often
    being closed.
My god, May God bless you, my
    dear, Goodbye.

●

THE ART OF LIVING

I behold you, LIFE, I love you,
Thou beauty, thou art on earth,
So marvellous, so precious a gift,
A fire-fly or an earth -worm, I be.

Each smile blooms roses on your cheeks.
Joy or sadness, each drop of tears,
Wonderful rain-bow with myriad colours,
With diverse blends, l draw, I erase.

A sun above, but multitudes down,
 Each grass-tip, with morning dew-drops bear.
And I enslaved with your beauty, sublime,
Boundless joy, this Art, this Life fills me.

This squirrel, tasting a nut, at the branch,
That "Touch-Me- Not " with a pretty squabble,
Touching the frost, my tender fingers,
Teaching me your pleasures, MY LOVE.

"Child is the father of the man ", the great poet.
But my child-hood, joyful, often tearful,
Still teach me the fine ART OF LIVING,
Though white-beard now, let I be a child.

●

MY FACEBOOK

1

Hi, this Facebook, how wonderful ! how nice !
Hi, this Facebook, how amazing ! how nice !
Till last evening lonely I was,
This morning my friends, not thousand,
But five thousand, fine, very fine,
My friend-list full, now houseful,
Hi this Facebook how wonderful, how nice !

2

Hi, how wonderful this Facebook ! how nice !
Not only here, in this remote hamlet of mine,
But there, in the far away land of America,
Oh! why not? even in the Sun and the Moon,
Beyond there, even in Mars too,
I have friends, don't be jealous.
Friend requests still in thousands daily,
Handsome guys, beautiful girls in myriad,
"Miss World's too, not miss even one.
Followers too not to count, who will ?
Likes after likes, comments after comments,
Thanks after thanks, my index finger, now broken.
Hi this Facebook, how wonderful, how nice ?

3

My neighbour, face to face a stranger to me, always,
He too like me, like my profile in the Facebook .
My wife, too beautiful, say my neighbours,
Yet I don't feel so this noon too.
Late last night, a charismatic profile I liked,
A Cleopatra in all sense, the beauty of my dreams,
Not only a ten likes, but a friend request too I tender,
My innocently innocent wife, she will not know, I hope,
But next morning, my wife's reply, "we are friends now",
I mistook her beautified profile and liked !!!
Hi, this Facebook how wonderful, how nice ?

4

Late at night weary of my full in full friend-list,
I deleted her, my wife from my friend-list,
And send a friend request to Him, the Almighty,
With a comment in Messenger too,
"Did you forget to create the Facebook at FIRST,
Had it been there, the Eve would never tempt,
Never tempt even to touch the Forbidden Fruit,
But that happened, why to complain now ? "
And a special request too to the Almighty I send,
"Please arrange the Facebook in the Heaven,
And in the Hell too please, it is a must there,
No wife, O. K, but no WI FI, never, please never,
Can adjust even without Oxygen,
But I can't without the Facebook, please,
Thanks a lot, my God, Thanks a lot,
Don't forget my request, please don't forget".
Hi, how wonderful this Facebook, how nice.
●

TRANQUILITY

A gentle breeze, down to the stream, below,
On lovely ripples, above the under-currents!
No sounds, no furies !!
Only me, a tender leaf,
And the blue sky above !!!
Miles and miles !!!!
In to the highest depths of tranquillity !!!!!
Ecstasy of eternal tranquillity ,!!!!!!
My joy for ever, My joy for ever !!!!!!!.

●

PRICELESS, HER PRIDE

"Please pack up your beloved belongings, my dear,
It is the time to depart from this home, to the abode so far ".
Murmuring of my ever-time, ever-loving life mate,
Who followed me with my shadow always,
His foot-prints with my each footstep up the hills, down the valleys.
Whether sweet or bitter, day or night nevertheless.

What is so precious to me my bewildered eyes,
Search each nook and corner, light and darkness,
Each page of my Account book from birth to last breath,
What is priceless, which is precious, my eyes faint.
My romance? My sweetheart? My dad? My son?
Or my so boasted, so boosted motherhood?
This blue gems, his precious wedding gift?
Or my so preserved and long cherished virginity?
My pyre lit, flaming flames kiss my tender feet,
Which or what to take with me to the. Heavenly abode ???
"Just a second my dear let me take it from this dark corner,
It is not worn out by time, not torn out by termites.
Here, at this corner lies left my womanhood,
My most precious identity, just a second, let me take it".

●

THE CARPENTER

1

An ordinary, but grand old man,
With long, white, husky beard,
At the fag end of his sixties, yet in haste,
His left hand, always his spectacle,
Both in vision and mission alike.
Like his noble father he too a carpenter,
This craft his ancestoral profession.
A hapless fellow, born to make wooden roofs,
For countless villagers, both rich and poor,
But the magic fate left him with no roof of his own.

2

Yet the fate showered blessings to him in rich,
With nine children, five his own gender,
Five little carpenters, no school in his hamlet,
He himself their school, college and university,
His skill and craft, their syllabus and curriculum,
Learning a lot, but earning a little,
All the five left him, and the village too,
In search of greenest pastures in adjacent villages,
Leaving the old man and his frail old lady,

She too in her sixties, a pity picture,
With no bread, no butter, in the twilight of life.

3

Though old and hapless a carpenter,
His frame lean and frail, yet,
Still young and vigorous on the roofs,
His only capital, at this petty old age too,
Still his shadows black under all the roofs he mended,
He mended roofs for all, but not for him,
From errors to errors, spelled his doom,
All nights spilled over with dreams so sweet,
To awake with their own roof, the next morning,
But the merchant of fate left him no room.

4

The last night with so fierce a hurricane,
Washed away all the dreams they cherished for long,
And their outdoor hut with dry-grass roof too.
His eyes shut, his lips frozen, the white beard wet,
His soul abode, in search of his ancestral home,
Home for all, but not for him, the hapless carpenter,
Home for all, homeless a carpenter, a magic fate.
●

TIME

You call it TIME,, but to me golden shore,
  Each second, a sand-grain each.
Picking them one by one, my labour,
Soaking with tears and melting with toil,
A gorgeous mansion, here I build.
You call it LIFE, but to fate a funny toy
To be washed away by the callous waves.

This riverbed, this desert, this golden shore,
Each wind sprinkles the tiny sand-grains,
But my children running, playing and sleeping,
You call them dreams, mirage ! or marvel !
They hurrah, never yield to your interpretations !

The wheels of that dark chariot, can never crush
This bliss, this shore, this sands of joyful grains,
For, they, glued with my unquenchable thirst.
●

MY UNBORN POEMS

This morning too bright and synergic,
"Good morning Papa, " Good morning Papa,"
Sweety, my seven year old daughter,
Kissing on my right cheek, as usual
And Hero my five year old son too
On my left cheek, both the seals of love.
Their teacher-turned hand-some mummy too
Follow the suit, on my forehead.
Six hands waving at me, in the school van.

My mood so hilarious up to the sky,
And my mind a singing bird,
Putting off my favourite football match,
I, to the court yard with a pen and paper
To strike down a few lines, as often,
Under the shadow of the green-wood tree.
The morning-rays playing piano in me.
All of a sudden fall of a sparrow
At my foot, a tragic fall from somewhere.
My mood out, no ink, no words, no poem.
With my stethoscope I too left home.

My receptionist under the golden board
"SUPERMAN'S IVF CLINIC " bids good-morning,

My patients, no my clients, in hundreds,
Waiting in Queue, with impatience.
A fair lady, she too a brilliant teacher,
Seven years in wedlock with her beloved,
God yet to bless them with a baby.
And in the Queue, a handsome young man,
A Pilot who ply war-planes beyond the horizons,
But his smiling dreams still on the ground.
Hundreds in Queue up to the dusk.

Sipping a cup of hot tea and my favourite football match,
My beloved beside me, and I in relaxed mood.
The invisible hand at Estadio Azteca[*1],
My hero, my Maradona strike the golden goal
And win the match amid reverberations of multitudes.

I too hope in earnest, an invisible hand
To pull all my strikes to the net.
But my hope still a wild fiasco,
Only forty percent win, as the Almighty's will,
All others leave my Clinic with empty-hands.

Smiling children make our earth an Eaden.
Their smiles, finest poems I ever seen.
My unborn poems, no more an agony.
My unborn poems no more an agony, no more.

●

[*1] Estadio Azteca is a multi-purpose stadium located in Mexico City where
Diego Maradona won the magic goal with "the hand of God" in 1986 FIFA
World Cup.